From my initial diagno͏̵ ͏̵the first CT
PET scan 6 months aft͏̵ ͏̵rgery I
chronicled my feelings ͏̵ ͏̵ ͏̵.....ᴇ in
poetry in the hope that my journey
might help others battling cancer.

Diagnosis – T4aN3bM0 squamous cell
carcinoma of the larynx.

Original prognosis October 2022 –
Without treatment 6 months life
expectancy, with treatment 45% of
living over 5 years.

Treatment – Total laryngectomy,
bilateral neck dissection December
2022 followed by adjuvant
chemoradiotherapy completed in
March 2023.

With grateful thanks to my surgeon,
oncologist the doctors, and all the
nurses, general, district, dieticians,
speech therapists & Macmillan in the

Northern Care Alliance who helped me throughout my journey.

I apologise for any offence caused by any of the following, the poems were written at the time when feelings were raw.

Never surrender when there is a glimmer of hope

#FCUKCANCER

Warwick Smith

Had better days

The last 24 hours have been a haze,
It's true I've had better days.
"Come in, sit down", says the doctor so solemnly,
And immediately you know it's gone wrong so
horribly.
"I have some news and it's not good".
"I'd make it easier if only I could".
"I'm so sorry there's no easy way to say".
"Cancer has snared you and is trying to take you
away".

"What is the prognosis?", I ask, with some dread.
"How long have I got before I am dead?".
"Take no action & 6 months at best,
But there is a chance if you're up for the test".
"I can cut your throat from ear to ear,
But let me make it perfectly clear",
"Your voice box will go, both lymph nodes too,
And there are risks and not just a few".
"Heart attack, stroke, clots & infection,
Could happen in the surgery dissection",
"Followed by 2 weeks in ICU,
The following could happen to you".
"Pneumonia, MRSA & covid of course,
It really couldn't be any worse".
"But if you get through & the Cancer doesn't
advance,
You will have a fighting chance'"
"45% of living 5 years".
And I think to myself, well that's a few beers,

I'll give it a go, I'm a fighting man,
Please everybody, look out for my Ann.
I hope to see you on the other side,
Because from a fight I've never shied.
The next few weeks may be a daze,
But hopefully I'll have better days.

By Warwick Smith
4/11/22

Shock

Bit of a shock hearing six months to live,
Thought I had so much more to give.
Cancer happens to other people not me,
Besides, who else can make my Anns' tea?
I want to watch the grandkids grow up,
Besides there's a few more beers to sup.
5 days to go to my major op,
Detox tomorrow so today's the last day on the pop.
Family and friends have been a great support,
But I may have to cut down from 'eleventeen' pints
to a quart.
At least I'll shed a few pounds,
And maybe I can again visit Leeds United's
hallowed ground.
So, keep sending those positives vibes,
And I hope to continue responding with witty jibes.
A successful op will add years to my life,
To enjoy more boozy holidays with my loving wife.
I'll battle through this, have no fear,
And if you're reading this; after the op, you owe me
a beer.

By Warwick Smith
27/11/22

Today

Today is the last day of my current life,
Trying to relax before the oncoming strife.
Spending the day doing things taken for granted,
Before my new breathing device is implanted.
Maybe I should sing songs of my favourite choice,
Whilst I still have my current voice.
Smelling sweet smells through my nose,
Before that airway is forever closed.
My last few yawns with wide open mouth,
As tomorrow that option goes due south.
Spending the day eating chocolate, jelly sweets &
cola cubes,
As I'll be fed for a week up my nose through tubes.
Maybe I should practise my handwriting a tad,
As the only way to communicate for a few days will
be with a notepad.
Perhaps I should send up a quick prayer,
For a blessing to get well quick whilst in intensive
care.
I might go in the garden for one last spit,
But at least I'll never have another sneezing fit.
I'll end now, I maybe offline for a while,
So, I'll end this poem by hopefully giving you a
smile.
As I guess there are more things I'll miss - so let's
pretend,
Like imaginary dreams of a bog snorkelling world
record coming to an end.

By Warwick Smith
1/12/22

#FCUCKCANCER

F. orward I walk into the fight
U. nless my time's up I'll be right
C. ounting on seeing you all again
K. icking cancers arse is my aim

C. ertainly I'm a tad wary
A. nd the op is a bit scary
N. o doubt I'll miss a beer
C. oz suppin ale could've been a career
E. ventually I'll be back on my feet
R. aring to go, I'll not accept defeat

By Warwick Smith
2/12/22

- waiting for cancer op on the date I was
considering retirement (read first letters
downwards)

ICU

Woke up in ICU with a canula, a catheter, 2 drains,
a nose tube & a neck stoma,
So that's the end of the operating drama.
I'm still alive so that's a bit of a bonus,
So, recovering is now my priority onus.
1 to 1 care with such a dedicated ICU nurse,
Managing the agony of pain, but I will overcome
that curse.
Every few millimetres holding my scar together is a
metal clip,
About 40 from ear to ear like a shiny new zip.
Movement is impossible without excruciating pain,
Only days of drugs & time will make it wain.
Washed, medicated & suctioned each day,
As time passes the pain did subside I have to say.
Out of bed, sat in a chair,
I feel my chances have gone up from poor to fair.
I thought my challenges were over but here comes
another,
Infection in the neck swollen so much I look like
Jabba the Hutts chubbier brother.
So that's a few days recovery thrown into the mix,
Whilst I'm pumped full of antibiotics.
Onto a general ward after a few days,
Transported still in a bed through this hospital
maze.
Temp, pulse, O2 & BP taken every few hours,
We should all make the most of this one life of ours.
Regular meds & fed through my nose tube,
And learning to clean & change my own neck tube
coated in lube.
The hardest thing is lifting my head,
Feels like I'm wearing a policeman's helmet filled
up with lead.

Over two days the chest drains, canula & catheter
are taken out,
Removal is far from painless have no doubt,
The next two days procedure is removing the staple
clips,
With what looks like a pair of Tin snips.
Now I target walking further each day & up the
amount of my exercise,
Trying to improve mind, body & soul, I could win
the hospital corridor callisthenics prize.
Visited regular by specialist nurses,
Don't you dare diss them or you'll feel the wrath of
my curses.
Just one final health test to pass,
Drinking radioactive fluid from a glass.
The swallow test to ensure there isn't a leak,
Alas there is, so my freedom is delayed by a week.
Once I pass that I'll start eating & drinking
normally again,
And then in a few days, out of here & my freedom
I'll regain.
There have been many tears along this tortuous
route,
But I'm getting there & will soon be back in my
local, although after 2 beers I'll be 'nissed as a
pewt'.

By Warwick Smith
13/12/22

Highs n Lows

Off we race to x-Ray in a wheelchair,
Oh! the excitement I just can't bear.
Only need to get the radioactive water drunk,
I'm sure the hole in my neck must by now have
shrunk.
I feel nothing but joy & elation,
That I'll soon leave behind this hospital situation.
Can't remember the last time I was so excited,
When they say I can go home I'll be extremely
delighted.

But alas the results are not so good,
The hole in my neck hasn't fully healed as it should.
My hopes have all come tumbling down,
There's nothing that can hide my disappointed
frown.
My morale has again run aground,
Feelings of hope & despair giving me the
runaround.

From a high to a low in a few seconds,
And I know depressions despair beckons.
So, I'll sulk for day and then drag myself up,
And then focus on that next fluoroscopy cup.
Fate you've picked the wrong guy to annoy,
I WILL have the rest of my life to enjoy.
I'll humour you & wait another week,
But I will be out of here when my body's healed the
leak.
Karma works in wondrous ways,
And I am looking forward to plenty of Happy Days.

By Warwick Smith
19/12/22

Hear me

Just because I have no voice,
Doesn't mean you have no choice,
To understand what I say,
I know I might not be clear as day,
But please don't just guess,
It only adds to my stress.
Even when I write things down,
Don't just glance & frown,
Please read carefully & check your understanding
with me,
Putting some effort in is the key.
Let me give you this mornings example,
Of what I wrote saying what for breakfast I'd like to
sample,
"Please can I have toast with butter no jam", & so I
waited for them to proceed,
Then they ask me, "Do you want jam?" FOR GODS
SAKE CAN YOU NOT READ?
Drives me crazy everyone listens but nobody hears,
It translates as contempt and drives me to tears.

By Warwick Smith
22/12/22

Christies - Is this the way to Radiochemo?

Welcome to the world famous Christie's cancer hospital,

We will do our best to get rid of your disease little by little.

Today we'll inject you with something radioactive, I know it doesn't sound very attractive.

But it helps us ensure your kidneys can take the test And that you will survive the radiotherapy quest.

Now let's talk about your treatment to come, It may sound a tad overpowering for some.

But this is what's happening in the coming 6 week, I'm afraid it does sound rather bleak.

Radiotherapy direct to your neck for 30 consecutive weekdays,

And there may well be side effects from these burning rays.

Kidney failure, clotting, burning of the throat and tinnitus,

Loss of taste, swallowing difficulties, and bone brittleness.

Heard it all before & it'll soon be over, to myself I think,

But then what I hear next makes my heart sink.

The doctor explains that running alongside this tortuous path,

Will be 6 weekly chemo sessions & I think you're having a laugh.

But the doctor explains it boosts my chances of lasting 5 years by 5%,

So, I'll take that as it raises my chances to 50/50 in any event.

So now to the pharmacy we head,

To pick up yet more prescriptions because I'll never surrender let it be said.

By Warwick Smith
19/1/23

Josie

Here I am in hospital feeling all safe & cosy,
The main reason due to a lovely nurse named Josie.
Heritage from Oldham, she's salt of the Earth this
Geordie lass,
One of the few with exceptional nursing class.
God broke the mould of solid gold that made this
special nurse,
And she alone has put my pain in reverse.
A bedside manner above the rest
We all love our Rosie coz she's the best

By Warwick Smith
10/2/22

As time goes by

A week in to the 6 week plan,
I'm trying to beat big C with all I can.
30 sessions of radiotherapy, one on every week day,
With a double whammy of chemo thrown in on a
Monday.
One week in & around 16% of RT done,
But this journey is far from fun.
Head clamped down in a plastic mask,
Receiving radiation is an arduous task.
Each day the soreness & pain increases,
The intensity never decreases.
One week after the first chemo session,
Side effects show with such aggression.
My kidney function plummets to 39%,
Any chemo today & my kidneys would be spent.
So first the plan is to massively rehydrate,
Intravenous fluids at a steady rate.
But now my blood pressure has more than doubled,
You could say my body is a little troubled.
Temperature rising throughout the day,
Is there no end to my woes I say,
Chest infection thrown in for good luck,
A challenging time has certainly struck.
Sent home with a strong antibiotic,
Let's hope that'll do the trick.
My treatment pathway I will complete,
Eat, sleep, drugs, draconian treatments, repeat.
It's a rollercoaster journey as time passes by,
But please let the reaper know I'm going nowhere,
It's not yet my time to die.

By Warwick Smith
Feb '23

No surrender

Week 3 of treatment has now begun,
After the Grim Reaper has had his fun.
Chemo almost wrecked my kidney function,
But now rescued after daily IV fluid introduction.
So after a successful recovery from my op,
And off this earthly plane I didn't pop.
The harbinger of doom played his cunning plan,
Still trying to snatch my soul if only he can.
After a week being on penicillin,
He showed he is such a villain,
As he made his plan for the kill,
Swelling, bleeding, hives & copious phlegm did indeed make me very ill.
Then the doctors discovered I am allergic that drug,
But with steroids I recovered so I'm still here you satanic mug.
Then with changing my meds my blood pressure has rocketed,
But my soul he's not yet pocketed.
A meds review is imminent & alternative chemo I start next week,
You'll have to try harder to snare me you deadly freak.
Coz you've picked on a stubborn old Yorkshire Tyke,
Who'll never surrender so you might as well go take a hike.

By Warwick Smith Feb 23

Radiotherapy GaGa (song)

I lay alone and watch your light
The intense beam in my cancer fight
And all my cancer from my past
It's burnt out in a radioactive blast
Your aim is so precise on my operation scars
But it feels like proton beams from invaders from
Mars
You give me pain & make me cry
I hope you really are making my cancer fry (radio)
So don't become some background noise
A backdrop for cancers girls and boys
Who just don't know, or just don't care
And just want the cancer burnt out from its lair
You now have your time, you have the power
Blasting out cancer is your finest hour
Radio (therapy)
All we hear is radio ga ga
Radio goo goo
Radio ga ga
All we hear is radio ga ga
Radio blah blah
Radio, what's new?
Radio, we secretly love you
We watch the beam, we watch the stars
Of radiotherapy for hours and hours
We hardly need to use our ears
The radiation never changes through the years
Let's hope you never leave, old friend
Like all good things, on you we depend

So stick around, & blast away
So I can be rid of cancer soon some day
Cancer you had your time, you had the powers
But now we near your final hours
Radio (therapy)
All we hear is radio ga ga
Radio goo goo
Radio ga ga
All we hear is radio ga ga
Radio goo goo
Radio ga ga

Warwick Feb 23 (sure Freddie Mercury wouldn't
mind my plagiarism)

Final Countdown(song)

Cancer & I living together
I hope it's farewell
And maybe it'll come back
To me, who can tell?
I guess there is no one to blame
We're leaving for Christie's
Will things ever be the same again?
It's the final countdown
The final countdown
Oh
We're headin' for Christies
And I stand tall
'Cause radiotherapy is next
And killing cancer is the call, yeah
With only 15 radio beams to go
And cells to be hit (to be hit)
I'm sure that they'll clear, so
It's the final countdown
The final countdown
The final countdown (final countdown)
(Oh)
Oh

By Warwick Smith
Feb 23

Final slog

The last week of treatment lies ahead,
And I take a breath in with both joy and dread.
It's been a tortuous journey since recovering from the operation,
Travelling down the road of 6 weeks radiation.
Each day it's fired at my neck,
To kill off the cancer & keep infection in check.
It burns the skin both outside and in,
With just a gentle tingle to begin.
Lashings of creams applied to the outside of my neck each day,
And constantly sipping water to keep internal pain at bay.
Each session is not only a step up the ladder of health,
It's like stacking up tins of pain on the agony shelf.
Every day my skin tenderness increases,
And it feels like my gullet & throat are shredded into pieces.
The skin on my neck is indescribably sore,
And my throat can barely take more.
Swallowing now is now nigh on an impossible thing,
Plus the pain is so excruciating.
But I stand tall heading into the last week of the fight,
As at the end of the tunnel I can see the light.
Five radio sessions & 1 chemo to go,
Then I've completed this nuclear show.
So if it's liquids only so let it be,
I got your card marked cancer just watch & see.

By Warwick Smith
5/3/23 in f@#<ing agony

Ring my bell

I feel laughter lines creasing my face as the bell ringer,
As I forget the suffering as I went thru the wringer.
Just a simple task to ring a shiny brass bell,
For this right I've touched the gates of Hell.
My hand gripped tightly round the dangling rope,
Now I feel I can at last look forward with some hope.
Radio & chemotherapy have come to an end,
And I hope to the devil with every ring, the cancer to send.
The path to this point for me has been physically brutal,
I'm just happy to have won this draconian dual.
Now a decision on how to ring,
The choice isn't such an easy thing.
Is it just a solitary ding or dong?
Or shall I break out into song?
Maybe reminiscent of an old bus conductors ding, ding,
Oh! bell how shall I make you ring?
So exited I just ring it like the clappers as loud as I can,
And cry as I thank the staff and my Ann.
Without them where would I be?
So farewell Grim Reaper for now I'm cancer free.
And I can look forward to my retirement and a few more years, That's if I can stop these floods of tears.

By Warwick Smith
10/03/22

Singing the Blues

Another first for me and my lovely wife,
In the back of an ambulance with sirens & lights
flashing, racing to save my life.
It didn't take the ambulance no time at all,
To arrive at resus after our emergency call.
After a weekend of puking & terrible squits,
Didn't think I could do so many loose toilet visits.
But today I just couldn't draw even half a breath,
Never felt so close to an early death.
My breathing stoma was clogged and no air would
pass,
Oh what I'd give for a lung full of that sweet
smelling gas.
In resus in no time at all they cleared my airway,
And a tearful thank you was all I could manage to
say.
So off to a ward I was sent as soon as a suitable bed
was found,
After a day where in my own phlegm I near
drowned.
The Acute Respiratory Care Unit was where I was
placed,
As this was were the most suitable care was based.
With the ENT doctors words ringing in our ears,
nebulise. nebulise, nebulise,
This would be harder to do than you realise.
From around 1pm to 6 I sat on that ward,
Pleading for pain relief but was ignored.
In the end my wife brought my own meds from
home,

As those nurses just left me to fend on my own.

Never even saw a nebuliser let alone had its use,

The care was zero and there was no excuse.

Then again I could not breathe, and a few nurses acted as a team,

And into action came the suction machine.

The ENT doctor swiftly arrived,

And soon my airway was revived. Coincidentally the same doctor from that mornings resus,

It was then that we kicked up a bit of a fuss.

Seems the doctor didn't press the correct key on the hospital system,

So to the ward no instructions had come.

He was so apologetic and with it sincere,

But he could have cost me my life that I hold so dear.

Even ALL the nurses said they were sorry,

For us to wrongly experience all this stress and worry.

But I say wouldn't anyone with an ounce of common sense,

After 5 hours got off the hospital fence,

And just walked down one flight of stairs.

And asked the doctor why nothing had been received; or is it nowadays nobody cares ?

By Warwick Smith
18/3/23

Dishonourable discharge

(Part 1. Leaving hospital)

So a discharge from hospital is the best news all week,
There is nothing else I wish to seek,
But before I go there are some meds I need from Pharmacy,
And check the drugs are all there earnestly.
Just one item missing it's no surprise, Although with such a large order I do empathise.
The nurse then does her final checks, got all meds - Yes,
Got suction device at home - delivered this week, Yes,
Right you are all good so off you go,
Good luck with recovery, and take it slow.

(Part 2. Arriving at home)

Arrive home & sit down with relief,
And then look down in disbelief.
The suction machine is in pieces in its own bag,
And I'm now ready to wave the white flag.
No instructions on assembly or use,
Just left to fathom it out yourself I deduce.
So Ann hastily contacts the District Nurse to arrange for an urgent home visit
In the hope for some help to solicit.
The nurses are not best pleased & say I should have had training at home or in hospital on how to use this machine,
And maintain it & keep it clean.

Then the nurses step up a level when they see my
meds including solution in glass phials and then
ask,
Did you look after your own meds in hospital that's
quite a task ?
I replied, I did after the chaos of the first day, & it
wasn't a problem I preferred to look after myself,
I just set my meds out on the hospital shelf.
But then they asked how I opened the glass bottles
for my neb,
I didn't, any meds needing mixing the nurses did
and passed the mix to me in a syringe I said.
Well I'll ring the ward the District Nurse warned,
She didn't look happy and soon felt scorned,
The ward nurse said I had self managed the little
glass capsules, Was the ward nurse taking us for
fools ?
Apparently, you draw liquid out with a syringe, I
hadn't done this it was all lies,
And guess what there's another surprise.
Not even one syringe included in the pharmacy
pack,
Which means the District Nurses will have to come
back.
Training arranged for machine & glass meds by the
2 wonderful District Nurse gals,
And another email I need to send to Bury NHS
PALS

By Warwick Smith
22/3/23

Edge

Five months since my life changing operation day,
Now my life is so different in every way.
My working life was ended so abruptly,
It all seems so unjustly.
The black dog is now enveloping me,
And I feel there's no future I can see.
I have no voice and cannot chat as I once could,
And it's so hard to be understood.
No more deep meaningful conversation,
I so miss all the communication.
No witty banter in the pub
At the teatime drinking club.
No longer can be bothered with arguing the toss,
What's the point if I can't get my point across.
In the past I've been a coach, a trainer & a leader at
many a level,
And in public speaking I would revel,
I was known for spinning a good yarn & telling a
good story,
I used to revel in all that glory.
I've been honoured to act as a best man five times
in the past,
I loved making the speeches but now I've done my
last.
I can't talk to grandkids to offer words of advice,
And not being able to chit chat comes at a terrible
price.
No more whispers of endearment in a loving
embrace
And moments of passion have long gone in any
case.
To add to these woes I struggle to eat & drink,
And it hinders more than you think.
Can't face any outings to go for a meal,

Eating is now a chore & holds no appeal,
No more going to the pub & having 'eleventeen',
Because I struggle to swallow so I'm not keen.
 No more long walks because I cough & choke,
So my leisure time is now a joke.
I know deep down things will improve,
 But falling into depression it's hard to approve.
I plod on miserably day to day,
But have surpassed 6 months life expectancy from
October coz now it's May.
I know (& pray) that things will improve,
If only this black cloud I can remove.

By Warwick Smith(fighting depression)
May 23

April Fool

There's no bigger special day for me than today,
Because six months ago I remember the doctor say,
"Without the operation you have six months to
live".
And I remember thinking I had so much more to
give.
So the six month milestone has arrived,
And you may have noticed that so far I've
survived.
So lucky to have a second chance of life,
And I wouldn't have made it without the support of
my lovely wife.
She has fought this battle stood staunchly by my
side,
I couldn't have had a better wingman if I tried.
So the six month forecast seemed so cruel,
But we've made it, Grim Reaper, so you are the
April fool.

By Warwick Smith

31/3/23

Stay or go

Cancer you gotta let me know,
Can I stay or am I to go,
If you say that you're not mine,
I'll be here till the end of time,
So can I stay or am I to go.

It's always tease, tease, tease,
Cancer put me on my knees,
One day is fine the next is black,
Cancer get off my back,
Well come on & let me know,
Can I stay or am I to go.

Can I stay or am I to go now,
Can I stay or am I to go now,
If you say go there will be trouble,
And if I can stay it will be double,
So come on let me know.

The indecision's bugging me,
Esta indecidion me molesta,
So if I'm cancer free,
Dime rápida, y libérame.
I'll seize the rest of my life just wait and see,
Y apreciar todos los días

By Warwick Smith
June '23
 - with credit to The Clash should I stay or should I
go

Can't sleep

3am and wide awake, just can't sleep,
Today could be tears of joy or with sadness I weep.
To find out if I'm cancer free,
It isn't easy all this waiting for me,
In 8 hours I see the oncologist,
I feel so healthy, but is there a bitter twist,
Can I go out and celebrate and get on with my life,
And have a long retirement with my wonderful
wife,
Or is there more treatment I have to endure,
That would be dreadful and I know that for sure,
Or could the news be even worse,
And my life is to end with cancers curse,
Oh1 Grim Reaper I hope the last laugh is mine,
And the doc says, "You're all clear, everything's
fine".

By Warwick Smith
3am 15/6/23

News

The McMillan nurse phones to say you have an
appointment tomorrow,
Immediately I think good news or sorrow?
The appointment is booked for 10:45,
The oncologist will see me before his clinic patients
arrive.
Couldn't sleep at all that night,
Wondering what would be my plight?
Up at 3:30am & sat downstairs,
Oh! what a terrible state of affairs.
My nebulisers are all done and it's only 4,
I don't know if I can take anymore.
The plants in the garden all watered by 5,
Thinking how thankful I am to still be alive.
Drink my supplements and feed Nora Catty, our
lovely cat,
Glance at the clock, only 6 thought it'd be later than
that.
What will the news bring - all clear, more treatment
or prepare for heaven,
Surely it can't only be 7.
Right, might as well get changed & ready don't
want to be late,
All ready and pacing, still only 8.
All kind of thoughts racing in this head of mine,
Time to set off it's half past nine.
We arrive early at 10:15,
Might as well find a coffee machine.
Sat in the waiting room as the clock ticks in slow
motion,
My head is ready to explode 'cause full of emotion.
The appointment time comes and goes,
Stress levels rising as anxiety grows.
Then my name is called and in we go,

Nervous pleasantries as I say hello.
I've examined your scan he says without delay,
And says, "It's all clear", straight away.
For a second; I'm taken aback,
As the monkey falls off my back.
I'm free to live my life,
Finished with all the cancer strife.
Outside on the way to the car feeling all aglow,
The tears of joy began to flow.
I will after all see the grandkids grow up,
And there's plenty of beers for me to sup.
And now we can book trips away with our southern
mates,
Let's start looking at some dates.
Emotions exploding in my mind,
As the darkness I leave behind.
I thank family & friends for positivity & prayers,
And thank God that's it's not my time yet to go
upstairs.
The only thing that can now bring me sorrow,
Is the hangover I'll definitely have tomorrow.

By Warwick Smith
June '23

Thank you for purchasing my booklet & all profits will be donated to my local laryngectomy support group registered charity – The Oldham Quiet Ones.

Never surrender where there is a glimmer of hope.

In memory of my late brother Mick Smith 'aka' Michael Sexton who died of laryngeal cancer 3 years before my own diagnosis

Warwick D. Smith

Printed in Great Britain
by Amazon